The Anger Relief Manual

Regaining Control & Detoxing Your Life

Anthony Glenn

Contents

What does living with anger look like?

Imagine waking up and it's a rainy day — you hate rain, and you're already late for work. You get ready in a hurry and leave the house, already annoyed. Then you get stuck in traffic. You get mad. A granny crosses the street, slow as a snail. Stupid woman! A driver from another car honks at you. What a moron! Can't he see that you can't move?! A colleague at work left you his job to finish. How can someone be such a jerk?! And the boss — he's the hugest jerk of all!

Later at home, you yell at your kids because they make a mess and can't play quietly. It seems like everyone does nothing but making you mad. That's why you have to deal with high blood pressure, but no one cares! You have your own problems, but they expect, they want, they demand. And all of them are so stupid and careless that you have to think for them, too. People these days are useless!

Your health suffers. Your marriage suffers. Your family and relationships suffer.

Because everyone *else* is wrong?

Living with anger is like living with a timebomb inside you. You don't know when it's going to explode or what it's going to destroy.

It's not pleasant at all. If you are not aware that you have a problem, it may seem that everyone and everything is wrong, and all sorts of things make you angry all of the time. Something must be seriously wrong with the world if everybody's primary mission is to annoy you.

On the other hand, if you become aware of the problem, you'll realize that something's very wrong with your behavior. You'll notice that your actions have unfortunate consequences. You'll realize that you are the one who is responsible for your relationships being in such poor condition. It's miserable as well, but it's the first step towards change. And it's time for a change.

Being a short-tempered person is not an excuse for the tears on your loved ones' faces. Nor for being disrespectful to your parents. It's not a reason for lashing out at everyone, nor for your children feeling afraid of you. You surely do not want to be someone's childhood nightmare or for people to avoid you.

You don't have another life. Your loved ones won't be here forever. Your children suffer and will have serious issues because of your yelling. Your short temper controls you unless you start controlling it.

Not only do your relationships and social life suffer, but your anger poisons both your body and your mind.

How does anger affect your health?

Like fear, panic, and anxiety, anger triggers the body's "fight or flight" response. You feel that you're in danger, and your body is preparing to fight or run away. The adrenal glands produce more stress hormones, such as adrenaline and cortisol. The brain prepares for physical exertion by shunting blood away from the gut and towards the muscles. Heart rate and blood pressure both increase to provide you with more oxygenated blood. Breathing shortens and quickens, body temperature rises, and the skin perspires. The mind becomes sharp and highly focused.

Feeling angry here and there is not a health problem. It's even good for your mental well-being. Well-managed anger expressed in a healthy way may help you by forcing you to find solutions and make positive changes. On the other hand, being angry all the time is nothing less than toxic. When your anger is not well-managed, your body suffers. It causes a constant flood of stress chemicals and it provokes specific metabolic changes that may eventually result in many different health issues, harming your body permanently.

Unmanaged anger is linked with many short-term and long-term physical problems. Some of the most common include:

- Headaches

The ups and downs of adrenaline levels and blood pressure oscillations quickly lead to headaches, which interfere with your everyday life.

- Insomnia

It's almost impossible to sleep when your body is prepared for "fight or flight". It needs time to calm down and to lower the levels of stress chemicals. But if you have angry outbursts often, your stress hormones are constantly high, which makes you sleepless. Lack of sleep makes you prone to more and more irritation and unpleasant feelings.

- Abdominal pain, digestion problems
- Increased anxiety

If you suffer from anxiety, keep in mind that anger can make your problem worse. You should find adequate help for both anxiety and anger. In one study from 2012 published in the journal *Cognitive Behavior Therapy*, researchers found that anger can intensify symptoms of GAD — generalized anxiety disorder. This is a condition characterized by an extreme worry that one cannot control, and that interferes with a person's daily life. People with GDA have higher anger levels. In addition, resentment, together with internalized, unexpressed anger contribute hugely to the severity of anxiety symptoms.

- Depression

Depression often goes hand-in-hand with anger and aggression, especially in men. Numerous studies have confirmed this connection. Passive anger, which is contemplated but never acted on, is common in people who suffer from depression. Most psychologists agree that besides therapy, the best advice for those who suffer from anger mixed with depression is to get busy. Choose any activity which fully absorbs your attention. It may be a sports activity, gardening, dancing, whatever you like. The important thing is that it should be something which fills your mind completely and pulls your focus towards the present moment. This leaves no room for anger or rumination. And a bonus — when you're physically active, you can burn off the stress hormones that would normally prepare you for flight or fight.

- Skin problems, such as eczema

Skin is our shield, which protects us from the outside world. It's not surprising that all of our wrong attitudes against the world around us are reflected in the health of our skin. If you have explosive reactions, expect your skin to do the same in self-destructive ways — with redness, itching, allergies, and more complicated conditions such as eczema.

- High blood pressure
- Heart attack

Did you know that in the two hours after an episode of anger, you have double the chances of having a heart attack? That sounds scary, right? By doing nothing to get control over your anger, you put your heart at great risk. Anger is physically damaging, but the worst of all is the effect on your cardiac health.

If your anger is repressed, you are even more prone to heart disease. You don't express your feelings directly and do your best to stay in control of it. But your anger needs an outlet or to be expressed somehow. If you don't find a proper way of doing so, it will turn self-destructive. Overall, studies have shown that angry people generally have twice the risk of heart disease.

To protect your most precious muscle, work on your inner peace. Don't wait to lose control. Learn to identify and address your feelings. Well-managed anger — when you know exactly what's bothering you, speak directly to the person you are angry with, and deal with problems constructively — is not associated with heart disease, and is actually a very normal, healthy emotion.

- Stroke

There are many reasons why you may regret lashing out, but it might be even more dangerous than most of us think. Not only is your heart in danger for two hours after an angry outburst, but there is also a three times higher risk of having a stroke. You are more prone to bleeding within the brain or developing a blood clot during the two hours afterwards as well. The risk is even six times higher for people with an aneurysm in one of the brain's arteries. An aneurysm can easily rupture after an angry outburst.

The good news is that you can learn to control those explosions of anger. To cope with your short temper, you need to first identify your triggers, and then figure out how to change your response. There are many techniques that can help you, from deep breathing to assertive communication skills.

- It weakens your immune system.

If you feel sick often, consider if you're stressed and mad all of the time. In a few studies, healthy people were given the task of recalling an angry experience from their past. That simple memory caused an unbelievable six-hour drop in levels of the cells' first line of defense against infection — the antibody immunoglobulin A.

If you find yourself constantly angry, you need to learn constructive strategies for coping with anger to protect your immune system, aside from all of the other benefits. There are many ways to deal with it, such as assertive communication, humor, effective problem solving, or restructuring your thoughts. But your first act must be to calm down.

- Resentment can hurt your lungs.

Maybe you are not a smoker, but you could still be hurting your lungs if you're permanently angry. In one study, 670 men were examined over eight years. Their anger levels were measured using a hostility scale scoring method. Any changes in their lung function were examined, too. The results have shown that the most hostile individuals had significantly worse lung capacity.

This increased their risk of respiratory problems. The most likely reason is that the uptick in stress hormones, which are associated with feelings of anger, creates inflammation in the respiratory system.

- Anger can shorten your life.

Happy people live longer, can you believe it? If you think it's a stretch that people with positive attitudes live longer, you still need to understand that chronic anger shortens your life. Anger causes stress. Stress is very closely linked to general health. General health contributes to your lifespan. Many scientific studies have shown that people who hold onto their anger live shorter lives than those who have no problems in expressing their feelings.

If you're not comfortable showing negative emotions, then you should seek help to learn how to do so. Expressing anger in an appropriate way is a good use of negative feelings. You have to know how to protect and stand up for yourself. Learn to talk to others directly and to express your feelings and needs.

Why Are You So Angry? Where Does It Come From?
Possible Psychological Reasons for Anger

Situations are not positive or negative by default. We are the ones who decide if something is good or bad, according to our beliefs and points of view. Feelings of anger surface according to how we interpret situations. Triggers that cause anger are different for everyone, but it's common to feel angry in cases in which we feel:

- attacked or threatened
- powerless
- frustrated
- mistreated or our worth is underestimated
- that others don't respect us, our limits, feelings, or possessions.

Since people can interpret situations differently, something that makes you feel hurt and mad may not make someone else feel upset at all (perhaps they might feel annoyed or amused, but not angry). Don't think you are wrong if you get angry. Because we are all different and interpret things differently, you are absolutely right to feel the way you do. Simply accept that you are angry.

What determines our understanding and reaction to situations?

Your interpretation and reaction to situations depends on many factors. Some of the most powerful among them include:

- current circumstances
- past experiences
- your childhood and upbringing
- a result of transferring other emotions or your way of distracting yourself from something else.

Whether the cause of your anger is in something that's occurring in the present or something that happened no matter how long ago, becoming aware of how and why we interpret and react to situations is the first step towards regaining control. When you realize how you see things, how you react the way you do, and why, you are ready to learn how to cope with your emotions better, allowing you to discover productive strategies for handling your anger.

Current circumstances

If you get angry more often and more easily than usual, or you have angry outbursts as a response to unrelated things and minor causes, you are probably dealing with a lot of other problems in your life.

If something is going on that makes you feel angry, but you are not able to resolve the situation or to express your feelings directly, then chances are that you will express that anger at other times.

Anger is also known to be a part of grief. If you've lost someone dear, it can be very difficult to move on and cope with all of the contradictory emotions you might have. Anger is a natural part of the process, but that doesn't mean that you don't need help to deal with it.

Your childhood and upbringing

At the age of about two or three, we learn how to cope with anger. The problem is, many of us learned wrong methods. So as adults, we might behave like emotional two-year-olds.

Messages we receive about anger as children may make it harder to manage it as grown-ups, so how we cope with angry feelings is often influenced by our upbringing. For example:

- Maybe you didn't learn to understand and manage your anger because you grew up thinking that there's no other way to act out your anger other than by being aggressive or violent. This could mean you have angry outbursts whenever you're in a situation you don't agree with, or when you don't like the way someone is behaving.
- You may have been punished for expressing your anger as a child. Maybe you have been brought up to believe that you shouldn't

complain. That's why as an adult you may tend to suppress your anger. It becomes a long-term problem because you react inappropriately to new situations you're not comfortable with. If you don't find ways to release your anger in a healthy way, you might also become self-destructive, turning this inward on yourself.

- If you witnessed your parents or other adults acting extremely angry and letting their emotions get out of control, it's not surprising that you think of anger as something terrifying and destructive. It's possible you now feel afraid of your own anger and have problems expressing it because you don't feel safe. Those suppressed emotions might then appear suddenly, at other unconnected times, which may be hard to explain.

Past experiences

If you've experienced a situation in the past that made you feel angry, such as trauma, abuse, or bullying (either as a child or more recently as an adult) when you weren't able to express your anger at the time, you might still be feeling anger. Certain situations are probably especially challenging for you and can easily make you angry.

Sometimes your present feeling of anger has nothing to do with the current situation but may be related to an experience from the past. The anger you are carrying within yourself into the present, which seems irrational, may actually be at a level appropriate to your past situation.

When you become aware of this, you can find ways to respond to situations in the present more safely and effectively.

Conversion and distraction

Anger can also be a way of expressing many other feelings.

Maybe as a child you were not taught to recognize, accept, and express different emotions. Perhaps you were taught that boys don't cry, or super girls shouldn't feel sadness or show their weaknesses. On the other hand, anger is often considered a demonstration of power — so it's not forbidden for strong boys and girls, right?

Surprisingly, for many people, the emotion that is most often converted into outbursts of anger is a feeling of powerlessness.

Whether you are right or wrong in your anger, you feel a sense of righteousness. This is seductive and offers a temporary yet powerful boost to self-esteem — much better than feeling vulnerable or helpless.

It's easier and also more satisfying to be angry than to become aware of your painful feelings. When you are mad, you convert your helplessness into a sense of power and control. If you are used to this, you may develop an unconscious habit of transforming all of your sour feelings into anger. This is easier than acknowledging your feelings of vulnerability and dealing with them.

But it's not a healthy or constructive way of coping with the problem. Anger may distract you from the fact that you feel powerless, but your feeling of vulnerability remains on some level. Although anger may distract you from a problem, it can't make the pain disappear.

Anger generally has no power to address or resolve your problems and the feelings they provoke. But it can create a lot of new issues, and damage your health and social life.

Signs that there's more to your anger than meets the eye

- You find it particularly hard to make compromises. You have a hard time understanding the other's point of view. Maybe you grew up in a family where anger was out of control. Perhaps you have memories of how the angry person was the loudest and most demanding, and always the one who got what they wanted. If you were feeling vulnerable and scared, compromising might bring up the fear of being powerless again.

- You find it hard to express other emotions. Do you like to say that you are tough and in control?

You are not too sensitive, emotional, never shed a tear? Emotions like fear, guilt, or shame are strange to you? Then it's most likely that you are using anger as a cover for them. Those emotions are normal for everyone, and if you feel they don't apply to you, they must have been converted into something else.

- You can't accept that people can have different opinions. You truly believe that you are always right and get upset when someone disagrees. Other points of view might seem like a challenge to you instead of simply different perspectives.

Anger Management:
Recognize the Warning Signs

Although it may seem that you lash out all of a sudden, this isn't actually what happens. There are many signs that you are switching into "fight or flight" mode and you can notice the physical symptoms if you pay attention to your body.

If you are aware of the signs that your temper is starting to boil and can spot the moment when you're starting to feel angry, you're on the right path to gaining control of your reactions. This step makes all the other steps of managing anger possible. You'll know exactly when to apply the techniques for controlling anger that you've learned. If you happen to miss them, don't blame yourself. You are on the right track towards becoming more self-aware and more in control of your reactions. It just requires practice. Some warning signs that an outburst of anger is imminent are:

- raising your voice
- knots in your stomach
- muscle tension
- shaking
- clenching your hands or jaw
- feeling clammy or flushed
- breathing faster
- headaches
- pacing or needing to walk around
- "seeing red"
- having trouble concentrating

- pounding heart
- tensing your shoulders
- gritting your teeth
- sweating
- tight chest
- being snappy or defensive
- getting a "flash" of a bad mood
- anxiety
- being overly critical of someone
- temporarily losing your sense of humor
- feeling argumentative

Identify the thoughts or negative thinking patterns that trigger your anger

It may seem to you that external factors are to blame for your anger: the actions of others, your unmet needs, frustrations, or challenging situations. But the fact is, it's not about what's happening, but how you feel. A situation by itself can't provoke your anger. The way you interpret what happens and how you think about it is what makes you angry.

There are some common thinking patterns that trigger most of us and fuel anger. You can probably recognize your particular manner of negative thinking below:

- Generalizing

When we are upset, we often look at our life through negative lenses and focus on what we don't like, overlooking all the good things. For example, "You

NEVER respect my opinion. NOBODY considers my needs. You ALWAYS do that! EVERYONE behaves rudely to me. I NEVER get what I deserve."

Of course, *everything* seems frustrating and takes on catastrophic dimensions when you think like that.

- "Musts" and "shoulds" — obsessing over an imagined, perfect picture

If you are not flexible and cannot easily accept how things really work, but have a rigid opinion of the way a given situation should go, it can be very frustrating. Life won't always go as you think it should, and you'll have hard times if you get angry whenever reality doesn't line up with your vision.

- Mind reading and jumping to conclusions

If you have the super power of being able to read others' thoughts, good for you. But that would be a subject for some other book. On the other hand, if you're an ordinary human being with anger issues, this thinking pattern can create a lot of problems. If you "know" what someone else is thinking or feeling — that he or she intentionally ignores your wishes, disrespects you, or makes you mad — you jump to conclusions. This is one type of irrational thinking.

- Collecting straws

You overlook anything positive in your present or the past, and instead search for anything to get upset about. You collect small irritations and let them build and build until you reach the "final straw". That's when you explode, usually over something unrelated and pretty minor.

- Blame

It's always someone else's fault. If you blame others for your problems instead of taking responsibility for your own life, you are actually putting your power in someone else's hands. Then you get angry and blame them when you're not satisfied.

Avoid situations, people, and places that bring out the worst in you

As adults, we have to cope with stress. While this can't be an excuse for unmanaged anger and misbehavior, understanding how these circumstances affect you can help you take control and avoid unnecessary irritation. Look at your daily routine. When is the time of day when you lash out most often? It might be the evening when you are already too tired to handle your duties, or during the morning when you are most stressed at work. Try to identify activities and situations that trigger irritable or angry feelings. In whose company do you feel more nervous? Which places make you uncomfortable? Maybe you get into a conflict every time you go out with certain friends. Or maybe the traffic on your way to work drives you crazy.

Is there any possible way to avoid those triggers? What could you change? If there's nothing you can do, try to reframe the situation and view it differently so it doesn't make your temper boil.

How to Cool Down

Once you learn how to recognize the signs that your temper is overheating and can anticipate an angry outburst, you can prevent it. Many techniques can help you calm down and keep your anger under control.

Tips for cooling down:

- Pay attention to the physical sensations of anger.

Instead of ignoring what's going on physically and being consumed by your angry thoughts, focus on the sensations of anger in your body. Although it may seem counterintuitive, this often decreases the emotional intensity of your anger.

- Breathe deeply.

Focus on slow and deep abdominal breathing to get as much fresh air as possible. This will release the rising tension that fuels your anger.

- Get some exercise.

In the moments immediately before an angry outburst, your energy is higher than usual, and you're already in "fight or flight" mode, which means that your body is prepared for physical activity. If you don't want that pent-up energy to erupt into hard words and hurt someone, a great idea is to spend it. An energetic walk around the block is a great idea. Jump, run, punch pillows, do whatever it takes to exert it without getting into an argument or a fight. When you spend pent-up energy, you can approach the situation more calmly and rationally.

- Use your senses.

Focusing on your senses has the same effect as breathing exercises or paying attention to physical sensations, bringing you back to the "here and now". Use the relaxing power of your senses of hearing, smell, sight, taste, and touch. Listen to some calming music. Notice the sensations of different surfaces on your skin. Smell a pleasant scent that takes you to a happy place. Look at some nice landscape or a scene from your environment. The important thing is to focus on what you are hearing / smelling / touching / seeing / tasting. You might also use your imagination and picture yourself in a calm, peaceful place.

- Relax tensed areas.

It's often enough to massage or stretch areas of tension. Our shoulders are where all of the stress, negative energy, and worries are collected. We literally carry them on our shoulders. Roll and relax your shoulders, or gently massage and try to relax your neck and scalp.

- Slowly count to ten.

Or count to 100. Or count backward from 100. The goal is to focus on counting, so your rational mind has time and the opportunity to catch up with your feelings.

- Check if your thinking is rational.

When you start getting upset about something, take a break. Let yourself be still for a few moments. This allows you to think and to decide how to respond instead of simply reacting. Think about the situation and ask yourself:

- How important is it in the larger view of things? Will it still be important in a month, a year, five years?
- Is it really worth losing my peace over?
- Is it worth ruining my mood?
- Is my action appropriate to the situation? Am I responding or reacting?
- Is there anything I can do about it?
- Is taking action worth my time?

- Take a timeout.

It's not entirely true that timeouts are just for kids. It would be nice if you could give yourself short breaks during the most stressful times of the day. A few moments of peaceful time might help you feel recharged and better prepared to handle daily challenges without getting nervous or angry.

- Find possible solutions.

A wise quotation says, "God grant me the serenity to accept the things I cannot change; courage to change the things I can; and wisdom to know the difference". We can apply the same to anger. There are things worth our attention and things that are not. Even the things that deeply matter to us cannot benefit from our anger. If you focus on what mistakes you made, your attention goes in the wrong direction. You should work on resolving the issue instead.

Think about possible solutions for the things that make you angry. Turn off the phone if calls often annoy you. Close the door on the children's messy room. Schedule dates later in the evening if your partner is always late. Or simply let go of an issue if it's not something really important to you. This will bring you such relief. Anger won't solve anything and might only make it worse.

- Avoid "You" and use "I" statements instead.

To avoid increasing tension by blaming and criticizing, describe the problem using "I" statements. As anger is your emotional reaction to the situation, talk about what it provokes in you. Be respectful and specific. For example, instead of saying, "You never clean anything!" say, "I'm upset that you left a mess—it makes me feel distracted". That way, you are sending a clear message, avoiding blame.

- Forgive.

Don't hold a grudge forever. It's natural to be angry from time to time and to stand up for yourself, but don't allow negative feelings and your bitterness to swallow you whole. When you forgive someone, you are setting yourself free and releasing toxicity from your life. Forgive and forget all of the small and bigger injustices. Forgiveness can do a lot for a relationship. Even if you have nothing more to do with the person who hurt you and he doesn't deserve your forgiveness, do it for yourself. "Anger is a way we punish ourselves for someone else's mistake", someone smart once said.

- Use humor as an antidote for tension.

Lightening up a situation can help release tension. If you look at the funny side of things, you'll see that not everything has to be serious. Maybe humor can help you face what made you angry, and then you can realize how minor it is. Perhaps you have unrealistic expectations, and humor helps you to see that. Even if none of the above happens, humor will surely defuse tension.

However, avoid sarcasm. Although it may be misrepresented as humor, it's only an unsuccessful attempt at being witty. And it will only make things worse.

- Practice relaxation skills.

We already mentioned breathing exercises and relieving muscle tension. When your temper is boiling, you can use more than one relaxation skill. Combine them. Practice deep breathing, count your breaths, and relax your body bit by bit. You can listen to calming music at the same time, or repeat a sentence as a mantra: "Take it easy", or "I'm exhaling tension and I'm inhaling peace". You can even make a sound like "Ommmm", which calms you. Write in a journal, do yoga poses, give yourself a break to meditate — whatever it takes for you to be able to relax.

Express Your Anger in a Healthy Way

If a situation is important and worth your effort, you definitely should do something about it. And you should express what you feel. There are many healthy ways to express emotions.

Believe it or not, anger doesn't have to be destructive. If you channel it properly and communicate respectfully, it can serve as a wonderful source of inspiration and energy for change.

Dig out the real reason for your anger. Have you noticed that the biggest fights most often happen over something small and silly? But keep in mind that little things like being five minutes late or leaving a dish out usually are not the real reasons for an argument. There's almost always a bigger issue behind it. If you realize that you are becoming annoyed and furious all of a sudden, ask yourself, "What is behind this? What am I really angry about?"

When you identify the real reason for your frustration, you will be able to communicate your anger better. This will also help you to take constructive action and come to a resolution.

Give yourself a break if things get too heated

If you feel that your blood is boiling, move away from the situation for a while. Take your time to cool down.

Go for a quick walk, go to the gym, listen to some music, or focus on breathing. This should allow you to calm down and release tension and negative emotions. Then you can approach the situation with a cooler head.

Play fair, even in a fight

Although it's natural and healthy to be upset at someone from time to time, you don't want to break down your relationships. This is why you should be careful about others while you're expressing your needs and feelings. Expressing yourself while still respecting others — this is what it means to fight fair.

What's your goal: improving your relationship or winning the argument?

Winning a fight is not a very constructive goal. If that's what you want, ask yourself why. But if you want to strengthen and maintain your relationship with someone and make yourselves both feel better, that's what your priority should be. So respect the other person and her feelings and viewpoint. Avoid hard words that you might regret later.

Stay in the present

When you find yourself in the heat of an argument, it's easy to unearth negative examples from the past. Placing the blame for grievances from the past on each other will make things worse. Rather, focus on the present and what you can do to make things better.

Pick your battles

Fights are draining. Don't get into an argument over just anything. First consider if the issue is worth your energy. Plus, if you carefully pick your battles, others will appreciate you more and take you more seriously when you are angry.

Be ready to forgive

If you are holding a grudge and can't release the urge to punish the other person, it's impossible to resolve a conflict. Resolution lies in forgiveness and finding better solutions that are acceptable to both sides. Punishment can never compensate us for our losses. It only adds to our pain by further wasting and draining our lives.

Agree to disagree

Have you ever convinced someone about something in an argument? Neither have I. If you can't come to an agreement, it's time to let it go.

A fight takes two people to keep it going. Don't be that other one. If a battle is going nowhere, you can choose to stop it and move on.

Develop your conflict resolution skills

Your relationships with other people at home and at work can either benefit or suffer depending on the way you respond to differences and disagreements. They can create resentment and painful splits, or they can build security and trust. That's why you should work on developing your skills of resolving conflicts in a positive manner that will help strengthen your relationships.

Know when it's time to talk to a professional

When you put all of these anger management techniques into practice, they should help you resolve the problem. But if your anger is still out of control, if you are hurting others, or have problems with the law, you need more help.

Seeking help is not a sign of weakness. There are many programs, therapists, and classes for people with anger management issues. You'll meet others with the same problem, and it makes things a little less hard when you know that you are not alone. Also, you'll get direct feedback on techniques for controlling anger, which can be extremely helpful.

Therapy

It's hard to control your anger if you still don't know why you are angry. Talk therapy for anger problems can be a great way to explore it and discover exactly what's behind your anger.

You'll learn more about yourself, your reasons, and your triggers under professional supervision. You'll also have a unique opportunity to learn and practice new skills for expressing your anger in a safe environment.

Anger management classes or groups

Therapy classes or groups allow you to meet other people coping with similar problems. It's comforting to know that you are not alone. You'll hear other people's stories and share experiences, but can also learn tips and tricks that can help. For cases of violence in the family, traditional anger management is not enough, so it's not recommended. If you have problems with domestic violence, you should work on your control issues, and there are special classes for that.

The following are undoubtedly signs that it's time to seek professional help for anger management:

- You feel continually frustrated and angry. Whatever you try, nothing helps.
- Your temper leads you into problems in your personal relationships and at work.
- You avoid meeting new people or attending events because you can't control your temper.

- Your anger has caused you to have problems with the law.
- Your anger has provoked you to physical violence.

Anger with Others:
Is the Other Person Really the Problem?

We get annoyed countless times throughout the day. Most often, we blame other people for our frustrations.

They are rude, ignorant, untidy, boring, too slow, too fast, they don't do anything the right way, they irritate us, they don't care...

Obviously, they have to change or we will always be frustrated. But something's wrong with this mindset, don't you think? We'll remain frustrated forever if we adhere to this way of thinking.

If you decide that you have to react to everyone else, and everyone is wrong or doing something wrong all of the time, you'll always be hurt and disappointed. Humanity will endlessly offend you.

Here's the secret. They're not the problem. The problem is never in another person.

Maybe you don't like it to hear it, but it's true.

The problem is our reaction.

There will always be countless external events to be upset about. You can't stop others from doing what they want and being who they are. But what you *can* do is change the way you react.

Anger is like a virus — when you get mad, you provoke an angry reaction on the other side, too.

If you learn to react in a calmer, more peaceful manner, you will go a long way towards a happier life and better relationships. Furiously yelling at someone provokes a completely different reaction than if you act compassionately. An act of compassion will make the other side more compassionate too, and more willing to resolve the situation. But an angry outburst will only provoke defensiveness on the other side.

It can be annoying when someone tells you that you are the one who needs to change and to calm down. But for your own sanity, it's crucial for you to react peacefully. Here's a short guide on how:

As we already mentioned, when you notice yourself getting irritated, offended, disappointed, frustrated, angry — press pause. Take a deep breath.

Hold yourself back from acting. Taking action while you're angry is harmful. It can provoke consequences you will later regret.

Reexamine your idea of how others should act and how everything should go. If you are holding onto this idea, you have a permanent conflict with reality. It's an idealistic fantasy, not in line with reality, and holding onto it will keep you frustrated. You can try to change reality and every little thing that bothers you to match your expectations — but if you succeed, you'll be the first person in the history of humanity to do so.

Give up on your expectations. Change your vision of a perfect reality for the actual one in front of you. Your unrealistic expectations create conflict and disappointment.

Accept the imperfect, messy, chaotic reality as it is. Accept the person in front of you, and yourself, as human beings. Don't hold onto illusions. Rather, accept real people with their weaknesses.

Act with empathy

When you accept that humans are not perfect, you stop blaming them. Then you are free to respond with compassion. Accepting reality doesn't mean you agree with everything and avoid action. It just means that you have more understanding, you act appropriately, and you let go of frustration.

But what if the other person really is responsible for the problem?

You may ask, what if the people you rely on are irresponsible and careless? They must be the problem. You simply have to get mad when someone behaves like that!

Well, it can be absolutely true that the other person is careless or irresponsible. And, even worse, the truth is that it may always be this way. You can't change that. But the question is, how will you deal with it? You can get mad, yell at them, explode, have a heart attack — but that will change nothing. Or you can let go of your expectations, calm down, and act appropriately within this reality.

How to act if you have to cope with difficult people or handle conflict

We've already stated that getting mad won't solve anything. But what can you do instead? Once you've cooled down, you can think about the situation clearly.

- Express your feelings.

Nobody says that you should suppress your emotions and keep what made you angry to yourself. You should communicate, but in an assertive manner. This means keeping in mind that it's perfectly fine to stand up for yourself and your needs, but respect others' as well. Stick with "I" statements instead of placing blame on anyone. "I feel so," "It made me upset when," and so on.

- Always try to understand the other side and to be compassionate.

We are all human, we make mistakes, but we all want the same thing — to be happy. We try to do our best, or at least what we think is our best. Everybody does what they can, depending on their abilities and knowledge.

Nobody is here to make you happy. Their job is to make themselves happy, and yours is to do that for yourself as well. Toss that expectation of others into the ocean. Of course, none of this means that it's ok to hurt others in the process.

- Respect limits — other people's and yours.

It's healthy to place boundaries to protect your personal space, both literally and figuratively.

- Learn to solve conflicts constructively.

There are many ways to resolve a problem between two people. The first step is to talk. Honestly express what's bothering you, what you want, how you feel. And be ready to hear and understand what the other side has to say.

You may come to a compromise, find a solution, decide to cooperate in a certain way, one of you may give up ground for the greater good, or you might agree to disagree. You could also decide to end your relationship or cooperation, but what you must not do is hurt each other.

Mindfulness as a Cure for Anger: Find Inner Peace and the Outside World Will Follow

Working on your anger issues includes finding more peace and becoming less frustrated throughout the day. But how can we remain calm when our emotions have been triggered?

Unfortunately, we can't change all of the frustrating things around us, so the answer hardly lies in the external.

You may hope for:

- always getting everything you want
- traffic to be better, and drivers to be kind and careful
- things to go as you like
- people to behave exactly how you want them to (with extra kindness for us)
- quiet when you want it, and excitement when you wish
- being more disciplined and sticking to your plans
- your home or workplace to be perfect, orderly, calm, and pleasant
- world leaders to run the world as we think they should

And so on. But that won't happen. We can't control everything — world events, other people, even ourselves at times. Things just won't always go the way we'd like.

When things don't go our way, we get angry. Obviously, things need to change their direction. You can't solve the problem by trying to fix the external situation. Anger is an inner problem and resolving it has to come from within. It's your inner response that should be changed.

What story do you tell yourself to maintain your anger?

When we get angry, it's always because of something we don't like. It may be a situation in general, or someone behaved in a way we don't agree with, or we dislike our own actions. We don't like our reality.

This is exactly what happens inside our heads:

We don't like what we see — the way someone behaved, a situation, or whatever causes anger.

We immediately feel a short moment of hatred and a moment of pain follows. We're hurt that things went that way, they acted that way, or something else happened. Believe it or not, this hurt lasts half a moment.

Immediately after that, we react with a feeling of anger.

That's when we start telling ourselves a story about the situation, another person, or ourselves. It's our version, our story about what's happening.

The initial pain has gone away, but the story has the purpose of making the wound fresh and keeps us angry. We are repeating the story in our heads.

As you see, there is a part of this that's unavoidable, and there will always be some conflict between people. The initial pain is unavoidable; everyone experiences it throughout their lives. Even the feeling of anger that follows is a pretty unavoidable self-defense reaction. But then comes the part which is absolutely under our control — our reaction. And there's one more thing between the last two — the story. We can control the story we are spinning in our head. It has the purpose of prolonging and even increasing the anger. So we need to stop that inner narrative.

Understanding the story

Stories that we constantly make and spin in our heads are normal and natural. Creating stories around everything helps us to put things in order and understand the world. But although these stories have the purpose of helping us, they are often not that useful.

When you are angry, the story might be something like, "He's always doing that. I don't know why he has to do that; he must be selfish and doesn't love me. He never cares about my needs; otherwise, he wouldn't behave like that". Or, "Why does she have to criticize me, I was just trying to..."and so on. We all do that, even if we are not aware of it.

The narrative feeds our anger. It traps us in toxic emotions, separates us from dear people, and worsen our relationships. Plus, the majority of the content is made up! We are just guessing, making suppositions, and we do it from the point of view of an angry person. We can't know what other people think or feel. Once we've made up a story, we start to believe it's true. Then we can spin it around in our heads for hours, days, a long time. It keeps our pain and anger fresh and alive.

The first step, as always, is to become aware. The next time you start to feel stressed, hurt, or angry, notice the story. Pay attention to what you're saying about the situation you are in or the person you're angry with. Be aware of the narrative you keep replaying.

The stories you often repeat become your pattern. Every time you are angry, you can fall into your old patterns of anger and telling the same story. Or, we can learn a new approach.

Here's what you can do instead of spinning your disturbing story:

Notice when the emotion of anger arises. Notice if you are already telling yourself a story.

Turn your attention to the physical sensations of hurt or anger in your body. Observe them for a while. What do they feel like? Where are they located in your body? How do they feel physically? What kind of energy are you feeling?

Don't run away from unpleasant feelings; stay with them as long as you can. Don't hurry back to your story. Instead of being "in your head", be more "in your body".

Accept the feelings. Everything we try to reject and destroy grows. Your negative feelings are as normal as the positive ones, so they're not something you should get rid of. Be ok with your emotions — it's as simple as that.

Try to see the bright side of your pain. *Which bright side?* you ask. It's easy to forget, but the fact is that your pain and anger are signs of your noble heart and basic goodness. Stay in touch with that positive side of yourself.

With this new response, we're turning our attention to the "here and now" — we are present and open to reality, instead of being locked within our stories.

We are changing our old pattern, a response we are used to, for a new and more constructive path, which is better for us.

Once you have stepped out of your narrative and you are open, you can try this:

Look at yourself with compassion. Then let yourself find peace, joy, and happiness.

Mentally turn to the other person you were angry with. See that the other person is also in pain, also struggling and fighting internal battles.

You are not the only one in pain. Other people have their pain, too. They react out of their habits and patterns, as best as they can. They repeat their own stories. We are all more similar than we think. Let this make you feel more connected to them. You know how it is to feel vulnerable, in pain, angry. Understand them. Even if a person is rude, try to understand her. From her perspective, maybe she's having a bad day, or even a bad life. It's not always about you. Everyone has battles we know nothing about.

Send them love mentally, forgive them for being human, and hope for them to find their peace and happiness.

Now, when your heart is full of compassion, you can take appropriate action. This may be having a meaningful conversation full of understanding and kindness, searching for a solution together, giving a hug, listening to their story and pain, or at the very least not being irritated and angry.

When you have issues with controlling anger, you usually respond too intensely and out of proportion with the actual circumstances. But now, from a place of compassion, you are able to take appropriate action, or even choose not to act at all.

Just as with learning any new skill or changing an old habit, this will require practice. If you continually practice, you'll become better and better at this. You'll have ups and downs, but move on. Every time you get mad, you have a new opportunity to practice this kind of mindful action.

Learn to respond, not react

Although we think we act consciously, many times we just react to events around us. These reactions are not always the best choice. They can make things worse and work against us.

Why do we do it?

We often react without thinking. It's a spontaneous reflex, often rooted in deep levels of our being, based on fear and insecurity. Most often, it's not the most rational or appropriate way to act.

On the other hand, responding means consciously deciding the best course of action, considering reason, compassion, cooperation, and other values.

For example, your child breaks something. You immediately get angry and yell, upsetting the child and yourself, worsening your relationship. You are not making anything better. That is reacting.

The other scenario for the same situation: Your child breaks something. Although you notice your anger reflex, you don't let it develop. You don't act on it. You press pause, focusing on breathing and considering the situation. The first response is to see if your child is ok. Second, remind yourself that the object that is broken is not that important (not compared to our loved ones). Let it go. It's just stuff. Third, help the child clean up — show her you are always there to help her. Make a game of it, tell her that mistakes happen and it's useless crying over spilled milk. Fourth, peacefully talk about how to avoid mistakes like that in the future. Don't forget to give her a hug.

This is the choice you have many times a day — whether it's your child being careless, your husband
not being kind enough, your mother annoying you, a co-worker being rude, and so on. Irritating external factors will never end. But you can learn not to worsen them by your reaction, and even to make things better by responding instead.

How to learn to respond

If you want to change your old way of reacting to events around you, you'll learn to become more mindful and to press pause. We have mentioned pausing and taking a break many times, but for this skill, it's crucial. You need to learn to stop for a moment and wait for the dust to settle.

Mindfulness should be your first step towards responding peacefully. When you are mindful and something happens that might normally upset you, watch yourself. Examine your emotional reaction. Observe how your mind reacts.

Then pause. Just because something happened and you have an internal reaction, doesn't mean that you have to act immediately. You can do nothing, just pause and breathe. You can notice the urge for acting irrationally arise, but do not take action. Just let it go. Sometimes it takes only a few moments. Other times, it's not enough and you should remove yourself from the situation to cool down before responding.

Watch the reaction fade away.

Now you are able to consider what your response might be. Think about it and choose the one which is the most compassionate and intelligent. You should respond in a way that will make the situation better, calm everyone down, teach others, help the relationship, and build better cooperation.

Again, as with all good habits, responding requires practice.

You'll surely mess up at least a few times, but in time, you'll get better. Try to be more mindful every time something triggers your anger. Remind yourself to pay attention when that happens again.

Refuse to engage

As the saying goes, it takes two to tango. A fight can't exist without you engaging in anger.

Practicing mindfulness, you'll learn that you are not what you feel. You'll become aware of your thoughts and the emotional reactions that follow. You'll learn to notice the storm is rising, but you're free to decide that you are not involved. You are just a spectator. It's enough to stay calm and do what we already said — don't take any action before everything settles down, calm yourself, and focus on breathing and the sensations in your body. Take a walk, do a short meditation. Peacefully watch the dark clouds, and the storm that's coming. But if you stay calm and in a safe place, you'll see the clouds dissipate and the storm will never take shape. No damage, no pain, no broken trees. The sky is clear again, the sun is shining, and the birds are singing. All because you decided not to take part in your internal storm.

Printed in Great Britain
by Amazon